... other adults who
... he illustrative explanations
...ation in this book will have direct effect
... lay practice, hopefully influencing a positive attitude
towards risky play.'

– *Martin van Rooijen, former coordinator of the*
adventure playground team, PhD researcher on risky play,
Utrecht, the Netherlands

'As Training Manager for QCAN (the peak body for school age care in Queensland, Australia), I am always on the lookout for information written in a clear, concise, relevant and easy to read format. Reading this edition of *The Busker's Guide to Risk* reinforced to me the need for a common sense approach to allowing children to experience risk. I would highly recommend this book to anyone looking for a realist view to approaching risk in children's play.'

– Joanne Jackson, Training Manager,
Queensland Children's Activities Network,
Australia

THE BUSKER'S
GUIDE TO RISK

THE BUSKER'S GUIDE TO RISK

Second Edition

SHELLY NEWSTEAD

Jessica Kingsley *Publishers*
London and Philadelphia

Contains public sector information published by the Health and Safety Executive and licensed under the Open Government Licence v3.0.

First edition published in 2008 by Common Threads Publications Ltd
This edition published in 2016
by Jessica Kingsley Publishers
73 Collier Street
London N1 9BE, UK
and
400 Market Street, Suite 400
Philadelphia, PA 19106, USA

www.jkp.com

Library of Congress Cataloging in Publication Data
Newstead, Shelly.
The Busker's guide to risk / Shelly Newstead. -- Second Edition.
pages cm. -- (The Busker's guides)
Revised edition of the author's The buskers guide to risk, 2008.
ISBN 978-1-84905-682-3 (alk. paper)
1. Risk-taking (Psychology) in children. 2. Child rearing. I. Title.
BF723.R57N49 2015
649'.5--dc23
2015019682

British Library Cataloguing in Publication Data
A CIP catalogue record for this book is available from the British Library

ISBN 978 1 84905 682 3
eISBN 978 1 78450 191 4

Printed and bound in Great Britain

Contents

Acknowledgement

With grateful thanks to our pre-publication reader, Anne Loat, Out of School Improvement Advisor, Kent County Council.

INTRODUCTION

Welcome to the second edition of *The Busker's Guide to Risk* – and for those of you who are used to these little books by now, I'm sure you'll agree with me that starting off with a few jokes is not at all out of keeping…so here goes…

Have you heard the one about the children who were banned from making daisy chains in case they ate them?

Or the school that stopped doing egg and spoon races in case a child dropped an egg and then turned out to be allergic to it?

Or what about the children who weren't allowed to play with cardboard boxes because they were a fire risk? (The boxes, that is, not the children...although any day now...!)

Risk – it's all a bit of a laugh really, isn't it?!

And there's more...(as that famous comedian used to say!)... Children who are not allowed to touch each other in the school playground in case it leads to a fight, children who can't play with toilet rolls in case they catch some sort of dreadful disease from them, children who are not allowed to play conkers without wearing some sort of NASA-approved protective eye furniture, children who are stopped from digging in the nursery garden because of the risk of e-coli, children who have elastic taken away in case they strangle each other with it…and don't even get me started on the subject of microwaving eggboxes…

Laugh out loud? Well, I would – if any of those were actually jokes – you know, like those urban myths that get passed around and exaggerated with every re-telling… But here's the punchline – they're not. All of those seemingly ludicrous things have really happened – to children whom you and I know, up and down the UK, in a neighbourhood near you – all in the name of *health and safety*.

But come off it, I hear you cry, this stuff is all ludicrous – where's your sense of humour gone, Shelly? Surely when those sort of headlines turn up, those of us who work in children's play can all laugh heartily at the fact that the world's gone mad and *those people* who are making those daft decisions really do need their heads testing – after all, we know better – don't we?

Well, yes, most of the time. And yes – sort of. Or maybe yes – in theory, but… And that little three-letter word is where all the trouble starts…*but*. And so for me, that's where the laughing stops. Because, folks, this is now getting serious. Deadly serious – and I really do mean that.

You see (and forgive me for stating the blindingly obvious here, but I do hope you'll agree that it really can't be said too many times), children need risk in their lives. Because if children don't experience risk, then they don't learn how to make decisions about risk. And if they don't learn how to make decisions about risk, then they can't take responsibility for those decisions. And if they don't know how to take responsibility… well, you can fill in your own punchline here – me, I'm off before that generation rules the world!

Don't ask me to prove any of this here, by the way. Not to say that it can't be done – it's just that you won't get academic research in a *Busker's Guide* (shame on you for even wondering!). But I'm confident enough of what I've said in the above paragraph to stand up and be counted. Even my grandmother, whose only knowledge of childhood theory comes from her own experience of having had children, grandchildren and, now, great-grandchildren, often talks about how her great-grandchildren aren't allowed to do things in the school playground any more and how this can't be good for them.

So if my grandmother knows this, and I know it – and, let's face it, we sort of all know it *really*, don't we – why do we, as professionals who work with children, sometimes struggle to do something about it?

Well, one of the reasons is because we're scared. We're scared of taking the risk that, by letting children take risks, something awful might happen – to the children, and also, if we're absolutely honest with ourselves, to us.

Those of us who have worked with children for a while now have seen adult fear about children taking risks in their play far outstrip the fear actually experienced by children as they climb trees, light fires and randomly wave sticks in the air (often surrounded by a slightly threatening posse of adults all crying *Don't do that, you'll poke somebody's eye out!*). Fear of children hurting themselves or each other, fear about *what the parents will say* when Johnny comes home with a gash in his knee, fear of legislation and fear of litigation are all given far too often as excuses for not letting children play.

But there is also another fear that we adults need to bring out into the light and give a good old airing – a fear which is so insidious that it often remains unspoken when any discussion about risk takes place. It's the fear that says *what if…* and sticks in the back of our heads as a terrifying possibility that might one day become a reality; it's the fear that says *not me!* and lodges in the front of our heads to prevent us from taking any action; it's the fear of *them*, those nameless, faceless authorities who tell us how it should be and what will happen to us down dark alleyways if it isn't…

You know *them* – well, actually, you probably don't. I say this because, when I ask on training courses, nobody seems to know who *they* are – despite everybody knowing about *them* and what *they* think… *They* are the people who say that children can't play with eggboxes, *they* are the ones who say that children must not play out in the snow, *they* make us give children 20-minute lectures on the dangers of playing outside so that when they do finally get into the 'environmental area' they are too scared witless to do anything that might be classed as vaguely interesting or enjoyable…

And yet we still don't know who *they* are…*they* have no names. Now that is scary.

But the point is (and this is truly terrifying – be afraid, be very afraid…), *they* don't actually have to exist in order to take the blame. Just the fact that *they* might be out there is usually enough to scare us all into clamping down on all those really fun – but ever so slightly potentially dangerous – things that children might want to do when playing. *They* is the term we usually use when we want to put the blame for not allowing children to take risks at someone else's (very securely locked and firmly bolted) door.

In other words, it's the fear of taking responsibility that prevents us from taking responsibility for risk. It's funny (or is it?) that in a culture where adults currently moan about children and young people being unable to take responsibility, we adults model so brilliantly how not to take responsibility when it comes to risk in play. There is a tendency to adopt not so much the precautionary principle as the nuclear method – stop children doing anything that might possibly involve any level of risk and then they won't get hurt and we won't get sued. Bad news for lawyers, no doubt – but even worse news for children.

Because what we adults who work in children's play need to get to grips with is that it's not up to *them* (those mysterious shadowy figures who might do something unspeakable to us if so much as one hair on Johnny's precious head is harmed) to make decisions about what levels of risk are acceptable for the children we work with – it's down to us. We need to do that stand up and be counted thing – face down those demons about what could, might, possibly happen one day in a very specific set of circumstances, and focus instead on how to take responsibility for allowing children to play as freely as possible in our settings – which means playing in a way which will inevitably involve taking risks.

The good news is that, as the Further Reading section shows, a lot more has been written about the importance of children being able to take risks in their play since the first edition of this book was published in 2008. Later in the same year, the 2002 version of *Managing Risk in Play Provision* was revised, with a further edition published in 2012 (see the Further Reading section). Endorsed by the Health and Safety Executive (HSE), the 2008 version of *Managing Risk in Play Provision* introduced the phrase 'risk–benefit assessment' to describe the process of weighing up the benefits of play against the risk of serious harm coming to children. In the first edition of this *Busker's Guide to Risk* I used the phrase *risk benefit analysis* to describe the process of assessing risk against play value, which had seemed to convince participants on training courses to think about the benefits of waving sticks around, rather than just proceeding straight to an automatic ban! However, now that the phrase *risk–benefit assessment* is widely recognised as part of the overall risk assessment process in play settings, I've changed 'risk benefit analysis' to 'risk–benefit assessment' in this second edition. (By the way, *Managing Risk in Play Provision* briefly mentions *dynamic risk assessment* to describe a process which I called *speed-of-light risk assessment* in the first edition of this book, but I think *speed-of-light risk assessment* has more of a *Busker's* ring to it, so I've kept it in this one!)

The other phrase that has turned up since the first edition is *risky play*. Now that's not something you'll find in this edition for two reasons. First of all, because, as we'll talk about later on, all play can be risky for some children on some level at some time in some circumstances, so really *risky play* is just play (as we know it in *Busker's Guides*, anyway). And second, what some adults mean by *risky play* is a form of adult-organised activity, perhaps better described as *adventurous play*. Providing activities can of course have many benefits for children, but it's not something that we playwork people do an awful lot of – we generally leave it up to the kids to decide how they play, rather than organise specific activities for specific purposes. So this second edition doesn't do *risky play*, it does *risk in play* instead.

Maybe at the time of going to print with this second edition of *The Busker's Guide to Risk*, risk is no longer the four-letter word that it once was in some settings – and for that we should be grateful. However, the battle against those demons I mentioned earlier isn't won yet. Well-meaning adults are still spending their weekends microwaving bits of cardboard so that children can play with them safely, and children are still being prevented from running in school playgrounds (honestly, I ask you – what else are self-respecting eight-year-olds supposed to do in playgrounds?!).

So, what do we need to go into battle against those demons? Well, a deep commitment to the importance of play in children's lives for a start, plus a bit of courage. We also need knowledge – and the confidence to use it.

So – *The Busker's Guide to Risk*, anybody? Could be a bit of a giggle…

Shelly Newstead

PS It's a convention in *Busker's Guides* that we don't normally use quotes from other sources – but given that this one is such an important topic with legislation to boot, it's probably better that you get the legal bits straight from the horse's mouth as it were! So anything that appears in 'quotation marks' comes from *Risk assessment: A Brief Guide to Controlling Risks in the Workplace* from the HSE, which replaced *Five Steps to Risk Assessment* (on which the first edition of this book was based) in 2014. In case you don't already have *Risk Assessment: A Brief Guide to Controlling Risks in the Workplace*, it can be downloaded for free from the HSE website – download it, devour it and learn to love it…!

PPS It's become a bit of a tradition with our *Busker's Guides* readers that they get in touch to tell us what they thought of the one they just read, how they used it, or even tell us some funny stories about things that have happened in their setting (which sometimes end up as cartoons in other *Busker's Guides*!). If you'd like to join in the conversation you'd be very welcome – get in touch at info@commonthreads.org.uk.

READY FOR PLAY

Chapter 1

RISK AND RESPONSIBILITY

Here we go – Chapter 1 of *The Busker's Guide to Risk*. You know how in some books you get a nice gentle lead-in, a few meanderings around the topic and a couple of case study examples to ease you into Chapter 2? Well, this isn't one of them I'm afraid, for two reasons. For a start, this is a *Busker's Guide*, and we haven't got the space to dally. And second, we're talking risk here and I'm sorry, there's no gentle way of putting this – some of us have been trying to give the topic a wide berth for long enough now!

So let's start by getting it straight in our minds what it is that we are responsible for. Actually, I'm going to get you to look at that question backwards to start with – what is it that we're *not* responsible for?

Well, for a start, people who work in children's play are not responsible for making sure that no child ever gets hurt. That would be just plain silly – because children have accidents, and when they are playing they can bump, fall, trip, slide and collide into most things that move, as well as pretty much anything that doesn't!

SEE THIS BRUISE? OH, LET ME TELL YOU THE STORY OF THAT ONE...

You've probably noticed how, when you talk to children about their play, one of the things that they delight in telling you about is the time that they *nearly* fell off their bike, or *nearly* hurt themselves. It's the *nearly* bit that provides the thrill, as well as a reinforcement of the child's ability to get themselves out of a tricky situation. Coming into close encounters with *risky* situations is sometimes part of what makes play fun – and also the bit that equips them with physical, mental and emotional skills to make decisions about how far to go next time. (We'll go into that more in Chapter 2.)

It might also come as a bit of a surprise to hear that we adults are not responsible for keeping children *safe*. Why not? Well, because safe means not dangerous, the absence of harm…and given what we know about the way that children play (see above!), we also know that trying to do away with any possibility that children might get hurt in our settings is simply not practical. The only way to really ensure *safety* is to have all the children in your setting lying down and wrapped in cotton wool (except, of course, for those who are allergic to cotton wool!).

So trying to keep children *safe* is just not practical – and neither, it could be argued, is it desirable (but that's Chapter 2 again and we'll get there soon, promise!).

'Risk is a part of everyday life and you are not expected to eliminate all risks' – which is, of course, music to the ears of those of us working in children's play. So children need to be safe enough in our settings rather than safe, because we work in settings which support play. So hoorah – everybody to the top of the tower for a spot of bungee jumping then? Ah – no, sorry, best not. The thing is, somebody has to make some decisions about what is an appropriate level of risk for children in your setting. Because what is safe enough for one child on one day will not be safe enough for a different child on a different day, or the same child on a different day, or some other child on a…anyway, you get my drift! And to be able to decide when something is safe enough and when it isn't, we need to understand some important phrases which are used in risk assessment: 'reasonably practicable', 'hazard' and 'risk'.

'Reasonably practicable'

So now we come back to the question of what it is that we are responsible for. And what the HSE tells us is that we 'need to do everything "reasonably practicable" to protect people from harm'.

Well, there you go then, there's your answer – really helpful, huh?! So over to you now, end of *Busker's Guide*!

But hang on a minute – because whilst at first glance that phrase 'reasonably practicable' might sound like it's going to be as much help as a poke in the eye with a sharp (-ish!) stick, it is actually really helpful to those of us who work where children play. Because we know that it's not 'reasonably practicable' to completely stop children from playing just in case they might hurt themselves (bring on the cotton wool bales!).

What is 'reasonably practicable' in our line of work is to try to strike a balance between the child's right to play and the benefits that play brings, and the possibility that they might, in some circumstances, do some serious damage to themselves, and then to do things which will help children to be safe enough in our settings.

The other reason that phrase 'reasonably practicable' is useful is that it reminds us that the decision about what is and what is not safe enough for children in our settings is ultimately down to us. What is 'reasonably practicable' for one group of children (or even one child) will be determined by all the things we know about the children, the environment, the types of play and many other things which could affect a situation at any given moment. Deciding what is 'reasonably practicable' in any situation will be influenced by your knowledge of all of these different factors, and your decision about what is safe enough will therefore change according to these differing circumstances.

Hazard

Let's move on to the easy one – 'hazard'. A hazard is anything which could cause harm. So if I imagine you sitting on a chair reading this book with other people nearby, the chair you are sitting on is a hazard (it could break underneath you and cause you some nasty bruising), you are a hazard (you might get fed up with me in the middle of this chapter and hurl your chair at someone in frustration), and even this dinky little *Busker's Guide* is a hazard (somebody might come past you in a hurry, jog your elbow and cause you to poke your eye out with it).

So everything's a (potential) hazard – you, the children, the equipment they play with (even the stuff that looks as if it couldn't harm a fly), the carpet on the floor, the air that we breathe…aaargh!!!! So do we shut up shop and run away as quickly (but carefully!) as we possibly can? No, of course not – just because something is a hazard doesn't automatically mean it's dangerous. Or to put it another way, just because something could cause harm doesn't mean that it will. Or to put it yet another way (bear with me!), it ain't what you do, it's the way that you do it…uh, maybe I'd better explain!

When we are working with children there are of course some hazards that cause us to do something about them straight away. For example, bare live wires, syringes in the playground, broken sections on the climbing equipment are all things that would cause us to immediately get out the gloves, partition off the affected area or perhaps even shut the site temporarily in order to make sure that children don't come to serious harm.

But then there are other hazards which only become unacceptably dangerous in certain circumstances. For example, clay up your nose or spread over the floor where someone could slip on it is a lot more hazardous than clay which is played with on a specific surface and in the normal way. Fire is not something you'd generally want wafting around your setting willy-nilly – but a few tea lights floating on a bowl of water in the middle of a seated circle of children, or a contained fire pit outside on an appropriate surface, aren't as hazardous as open fires lit in woods full of dry twigs.

TWELVE CHILDREN UP A TREE. THIS IS A HAZARD... THEY MIGHT FALL ON ME!

So, when we're thinking about children's play, we can't just automatically rule out anything which is a hazard. For a start, that would severely ruin your claim to be keen on children's play, wouldn't it?! It would result in lots of children all over the country sitting on the (squeaky clean – mind those germs!) floor, doing nothing. In Shakespeare's day, you know, all the world was a stage – in the twenty-first century all the world's a hazard. So instead of trying to remove every single hazard, we need to make judgements about just how hazardous those hazards are – or could be – and that's where that word risk comes in…

ALAS POOR FRED, I KNEW HIM AT THE AFTER-SCHOOL CLUB.

Risk

Slightly trickier, risks, because unlike hazards, they're not actually something you can get hold of. A risk is the measure of the likelihood that somebody might be harmed by a hazard. (Do feel free to go back and read it again, because I'm not sure that I can put it any better!)

What we need to get our heads round here is that a risk is a *judgement* about how much harm is likely to happen – actually, that's not a bad way of putting it! So a risk isn't a thing that exists by itself (on a roll now!), and it's certainly not a thing that needs to be eradicated at all costs – it's a decision we make about how likely it is that harm will occur and how bad that harm could be.

Sorted – I hope! So, if your opinion about a situation is that it's pretty likely that harm will occur, and if it does then it's going to result in some pretty nasty injuries, then that's a high risk. On the other hand, if there is a possibility that some harm could occur but it's not going to be that bad if it does, then the risk is going to be low. Removing or banning certain things may well be the right thing to do in certain situations, on certain days, in particular weather conditions, when working with certain children who are in a particular mood – or it might not. It really does all depend on your assessment of how much risk you think all those hazards might present.

Personal stuff

Most of us who work with children are used to doing reflective practice nowadays, so I'm sure that it will come as no surprise to hear that we need to reflect on some personal stuff at this point.

Why? Well, because we all have our individual comfort zones when it comes to how much risk we take in our own lives. But when we're working with children, we have to make sure that we recognise when our personal comfort zones are taking over our professional judgements about the children we are working with. Let me share some of my personal stuff with you here to show you what I mean...

I am terrified of heights. And it's not the sort of fear that is the *I'm-standing-on-top-of-Eiffel-Tower-and-I-feel-a-bit-weird* type of terror, it's the *I'm-standing-on-a-chair-and-my-knees-have-just-left-home* type of terror. So you can imagine my pure and unbounded joy when I turn up to a playground and there are kids up things. Up trees, up towers, up climbing frames, up platforms and leaping off them and climbing up the platforms again… On some playgrounds it seems that just about every child is somewhere a lot higher than me (no short people gags thank you!). And it's not that I'm worried about getting up there with them (because I don't, I'm not that daft!). It's just that when I look up at these children beaming down at me from their trees, towers and (what look to me like) other assorted instruments of certain death, my eyes tell my brain to panic. My brain thanks my eyes for this vital message and tells them to remain alert and vigilant. And then my brain tells my mouth to warn these children of the mortal danger that it thinks they're in…and that's when my reflective practice and my brain over-ride function have to kick in!

Because what my eyes are really seeing is that these kids are not in mortal danger. And my brain does know that really, because if they *were* in mortal danger, the looks on their faces would clearly tell me that they were scared and they wouldn't be grinning and waving happily at me. Kids who can talk to you lucidly and move about freely without being paralysed by fear are probably in control of themselves and the situation they are in. And so my reflective practice not only tells my brain to keep my mouth shut – but also to be very aware of my facial expressions. Because the more worried I look, the more a child will think that perhaps there is something they need to be worried about – whereas before I turned up with my fear of heights, they had very little to worry about.

In other words, we need to separate out our personal stuff and make professional decisions about the amount of risk which is acceptable for the children whom we work with, rather than using knee-jerk reactions which may be based on our own fears. Sometimes the two might turn out to be one and the same thing – and sometimes they won't, so we need to use reflective practice to make sure that we can tell the difference, rather than just dumping a load of inappropriate fears on kids that they don't need.

Team talk

Because everyone has their own individual comfort zones, it's important to make sure that there is a shared approach to risk assessment within settings. Teams need to have really in-depth discussions about appropriate levels of risk on a regular basis so that there is a consistent approach in the setting. This might mean of course that some of us just have to put up with the butterflies in our stomachs sometimes, but teams may also decide that the levels of risk are too high in some situations and to take a different approach so that there is less risk of harm occurring.

Responsibility

Right, now we really are on our way to Chapter 2! The end of Chapter 1 brings us back full circle to the responsibility thing. It is down to you to make decisions about what is safe enough for the children you work with – and what is not. Not very scientific, I know – not so much your high-spec computer program for risk management, or even one of those complicated rating risk forms, but more your old-fashioned balancing scales (you know the ones, polished brass saucers on long diagonal chains) to help you to weigh up the level of potential harm and whether the risk of that harm happening is worth taking.

But actually this shouldn't surprise us – in fact I'd go as far as to say that we need to cherish our old brass scales and polish them up on a regular basis! Our work is very often not cut and dried – children's needs change and develop all the time, as do our responses to these needs. Making decisions about appropriate amounts of risk in play for the children whom we work with is just all part and parcel of a flexible and responsible approach to assessing the needs of developing children. One size doesn't fit all – but we know that anyway, so all we need to do now is to apply the same sort of thinking to risk in play.

I guess the bad news is that cast-iron rules there ain't – final decisions about what is safe enough for the children in your setting are down to you. And the good news? Final decisions about what is safe enough for the children in your setting are down to you. And there's more good news – there's a technique which can help you to do that, and it's called risk–benefit assessment…

Chapter 2

PUTTING THE BENEFIT INTO RISK ASSESSMENT

Risk–benefit assessment is an important concept for those of us who work in children's play. Basically, a risk–benefit approach recognises that for every action we take, there is an associated risk. So in order for us to do pretty much anything in life at all, we have to decide whether that risk is worth taking, and that's where risk–benefit assessment comes in.

For example, I'm sitting here typing away furiously, trying to meet the deadline for this book. Technically speaking, I suppose there is a chance that I could get repetitive strain injury, carpal tunnel syndrome or other medical ghastlies that I don't really understand (and would rather not know about, if I'm absolutely honest…). But for me, the benefits of getting this finished on time far outweigh the possibility that this might actually happen – in other words, it's worth taking the risk.

Now, for us adults who work with children, risk–benefit assessment is a really helpful way of thinking about risk, for two reasons. First, because it reinforces the idea that everyday life is full of risks. Second, because it reminds us that if we want to get anything out of life at all, then not only do we have to accept that there is an element of risk in everything we do, but that we also need to make decisions about whether risks are worth it on practically a minute-by-minute basis.

And third (sorry, did I catch you out there?!), we work with children – who, it seems to me, seem to be programmed to take risks! Remember how in Chapter 1 we talked about how children will tell you about the time that something *nearly* happened to them when they were playing? Well, this is an essential part of learning about risk for children – so those of us working in children's play need to be able to fight for their right to party – sorry, learn how to manage risk for themselves!

In other words, we need to be really good at explaining the benefits of letting children take (what we have assessed to be) appropriate risks in our settings – and I hope the following will help…

Physical risk

Children need to learn about their own bodies and what they will – and won't – do. They also need to be able to find out about their developing capabilities as they grow – to work out how their bodies are changing and what they are capable of as they develop. Strength, balance, stamina and many other physical abilities are all tested and measured by jumping that little bit higher, running that little bit faster, climbing that little bit further – or, indeed, by deciding not to.

If children are not given the opportunity to use all of their bodies and to test their physical limits, they may become physically incapable of coping with some of the demands made of their bodies and knowing what those limits are. This could potentially put children in serious danger if they find themselves in (or put themselves in) situations in which their bodies simply cannot perform as necessary.

Or to put it another way, call me odd and call me quirky, but I would rather that teenagers were trying out their physical prowess in the managed environment of an adventure playground than on a railway track – because when they find out that they can't quite jump as far as they thought they could, at least on an adventure playground they've got a better chance of landing on a crashmat…

Social and emotional risk

It's easy to think about the importance of physical risk-taking for children (and even easier to see it in action). But children also need risk-taking skills in order to develop social and emotional skills. Think about two children who are arguing over a toy. Each of them is actually taking a risk by engaging in an argument in the first place (instead of just giving in). All sorts of things could go wrong as a result of arguing – they might end up not being friends any more; one of them might tell her friends not to play with the other one and therefore lose more friends; one of them could thump the other one; an adult might overhear the argument and the toy might get taken away so that neither of them gets to play with it; or that adult might even tell them off… So choosing to argue is a risky strategy which, to the child, must seem worth any of these (negative) outcomes. This is a real case of risk–benefit assessment in action – even small children can make the decision that they want the toy so much that it's worth losing friends over or getting told off by an adult!

As they get older, children have to learn to make decisions which involve weighing up risks and benefits in situations where social and emotional losses could be incurred. If I go for the star role in the school play and have to sing a solo, is it worth taking the risk that it could all go horribly wrong – or actually it might be all right and everybody will think I'm a really good singer? If I smile at that girl I fancy, is she going to think I'm an idiot or might we get talking instead? Play allows children to take social and emotional risks – which are not *real* because they are *only playing*. What they learn in these *pretend* situations of play may be useful in real-life situations where they need to assess levels of social and emotional risk – both as children in the here-and-now and as adults in the future.

And whilst we're here – what's the standard adult response to the arguing-over-the-toy scenario? Well, in my experience it's often the adult who takes all the decisions – and in doing so takes away from the children all those opportunities for learning about risk…

Learning about risk

Being able to make decisions about how much risk you are comfortable with, being able to weigh up the pros and cons of taking certain actions and behaving in certain ways (in other words, being able to make risk–benefit assessments) is of course a skill in itself.

As adults we all make dozens of risk assessments every day – it's just that we don't necessarily think about them in that way. We take the top off the milk in the morning and if it's been in the fridge for a few days then we make a decision about whether to pour it over our cereal or not – because if it's off then there's a risk that it might make us ill.

We make conscious decisions to vary pin numbers for credit cards and our passwords on the internet because we know that somebody could get hold of them and spend our cash. We give the dark alley a wide berth at night and walk home the long way round if we feel that taking the shortcut could put us in danger.

All of our choices – whether to smoke, drink alcohol, travel in various ways and to different places, etc – involve some sort of weighing up of the pros and cons, those benefits and risks, in order to come to a final decision about the best course of action. Play allows children to develop those thinking processes for themselves, and to test out different strategies for assessing and responding to risk. If you find yourself in a rough-and-tumble game that you feel has gone a bit too far, or are on an arial runway for the first time, you need to be able to weigh up the risks and benefits of the various options available to help you to decide what to do next.

A child might only have to make a decision about whether to jump out of a 30-foot tree onto two blue foam mattresses once in her entire life, but in doing so she will be developing and practising her understanding about her own tolerance levels when it comes to risk – how much fear she can cope with, what she needs to do to put those fears into context, how she can overcome her fears in order to get what she wants – or how she can accept her decision (and perhaps the reactions of others) that the risk is too high and she won't make the jump. Our tree jumper is not only developing social and emotional skills from what appears to be just a high-risk physical activity, but also learning how to assess risk for herself – a skill which could be useful (and perhaps even vitally important) to everyday situations in all stages of her life.

JAKE'S WAVING A STICK ABOUT – CRUMBS, THAT'S RISKY!

Risk in perspective

Well, I could go on about the benefits of risk in play –
but I'm afraid there's no more space to do them justice
in this little book. The good news is that there is lots of
evidence around at the time of writing, some of which
is listed in the Further Reading section.

But before we get on to risk assessment in our settings,
which can, let's face it, be a bit of a daunting topic, we
need to just hang on to the fact that being able to take

risks in play may help children to develop skills for use both now and in the future. There will of course be situations where the risks outweigh the benefits – but before we all get terrified into banning anything which might possibly cause harm, we need to remember to put the benefits into our risk–benefit assessments.

Now there's a positive thought to move on to Chapter 3 with!

Chapter 3

Risk Assessments

Just before we get started on this chapter I need a bit of a stern word. I know you haven't actually committed any misdemeanours yet – but better safe than sorry, forewarned is forearmed, etc etc. Because, you see, what I need to make absolutely clear at the start of this chapter is that it is not about how to do a risk assessment

Yes, yes, I know it's called *risk assessments* – but please don't let me catch anyone producing a model risk assessment from this chapter. Because as we already said, making decisions about appropriate levels of risk is a professional judgement which needs to be made within the context of your setting. All risk assessments must be 'suitable and sufficient', and you will find some helpful notes on what this means in

Risk Assessment: A Brief Guide to Controlling Risks in the Workplace. But (yep, you guessed it!), it is down to you to decide what 'suitable and sufficient' actually means in practice in your setting.

So sorry and all that, but I can't tell you what is 'suitable and sufficient' for your setting, the children you work with and the different types of play that might go on there. This chapter will talk about some of the issues you might need to think about when carrying out risk assessments, but that's as far as we can go here, I'm afraid, because at the end of the day it is you who needs to make those decisions!

So now we've got that over and done with, the first thing we need to be clear about is what this phrase *risk assessment* actually means – and what it doesn't…

Site checks

Many of us are used to doing site checks – walking around our settings with a tick-list-type sheet, checking off things that could be broken or dangerous, making notes about things that need fixing or even doing things as we come across them (clearing up broken glass, replacing a light bulb here and there) and so on. (In one setting where I worked we found a gun cupboard whilst wandering around on a site check – amazing what can turn up, isn't it?!)

But as useful as the site-check process is (especially when it turns up weapons!), it's not the same as a risk assessment. Or to put it another way – when is a risk assessment not a risk assessment? When it's a site check! (See, promised you a bit of a giggle – bet that one got you rolling in the aisles, didn't it?!)

The reason is that, when you think about it, there are an awful lot of hazards which don't turn up on those site-check lists (all the world's a hazard, remember?). There are also an awful lot of things that site checks don't include – visitors to the setting, trips and outings, specialist equipment or one-off activities… All pretty standard stuff in our settings, but all of which involve new hazards in one form or another and therefore 'might cause harm to people'. And that's even before we start thinking about adding children, and all those times when they do things in their play which we hadn't anticipated and we have to make split-second decisions about how much risk might be involved – but we'll get to that bit later!

Risk assessment is actually nothing more complicated than a clearly defined decision-making process which helps us decide 'whether you are taking reasonable steps to prevent that harm', given what is 'reasonably practicable'. And as we said earlier, we adults carry out our own personal risk assessments pretty much all day, every day, so it's a skill we already have. All we have to do now is to work out how to put it into practice in our settings.

I COULD GET A PAPER-CUT FROM THIS RISK ASSESSMENT FORM.

Don't panic!

Now at this point it would be very easy, wouldn't it, to go mad on risk assessments. Every piece of equipment, every activity…just where do we stop, I hear you cry?!

But hang on a minute – for those of you who are starting to gibber as you envisage being buried in piles of paperwork and never seeing a child again (let alone letting them play with anything at all ever), remember that risk assessments need to be 'suitable and sufficient' – and it's you who gets to decide what that means in practice. So by all means, if you feel the need to do a risk assessment every time you get the LEGO® out, feel free. Personally, I'd probably think that was overkill in most settings, but it's your call, remember!

The law doesn't tell us exactly when to risk assess, but you could ask yourself the following questions to help you to decide whether you feel that your risk assessments are 'suitable and sufficient':

- Has this thing/person/situation been risk assessed before?

- If it has been risk assessed before, are there now significant changes or differences from the last time it was done?

- If it has been risk assessed before, am I certain that there have been no significant changes?

This last question particularly applies to trips and outings. I've lost count of the number of settings who have told me stories about turning up at their usual spot on the beach at Bournemouth/Blackpool/Bognor (pick your own seaside town, preferably beginning with B!) with 40 hot and travel-sick kids, only to find that a sewage pipe has been built down the middle of their usual piece of sand (with the all-too-predictable disastrous consequences!).

So that's all fine and dandy then. There are lots of things in a setting which you can do a risk assessment on before the children get anywhere near the place. Your indoor/outdoor environment, the people who are going to be there, the activities that might be part of the sessions and the equipment that children will use, for example. Add the special events and activities and you've got a fairly straightforward list of risk assessments to carry out every day/week/month/half-termly – whatever you decide is 'suitable and sufficient' for each thing.

But then…drum roll please! Enter children stage-right…and now it all gets a bit more complicated, I'm afraid…

Speed-of-light risk assessments

And it gets complicated for several reasons. Not only because, technically speaking, children constitute a hazard in themselves, but also because, when they play, children will do unexpected things – things that you could not have possibly risk-assessed in advance. They may, for example, work out how to get the curtains down to use them to build a den (involving several chairs stacked on top of each other and using somebody's shoe as a hammer), or they may work out that if they climb up the (slippery wet rock) water feature with a bucket they could get water to make mud pies with. They may start to play a game that involves lots of children in large amounts of rough and tumble, or balancing on a gate which is not closed so that it swings when they are standing on it...

And this is where the really clever bit of risk–benefit assessment as we know it (Jim) comes in. Because clearly these situations all present hazards to children, they've not been risk assessed before in these particular circumstances, and so we need some form of risk assessment here.

But do we shout at children and tell them to stop what they are doing right now because we haven't completed the relevant paperwork?! Well, no, not normally, because we'd stop most of children's play in its tracks if we took that approach! What we can do instead is a *speed-of-light risk assessment* in our heads which takes place very quickly and sounds something like this:

- What could cause her harm? (*the hazards*)

- How much harm is she (and/or others) likely to come to? (*the risk*)

- What benefits could the child be getting out of playing in that way?

- Is there anything I could do to reduce the risk?

- Weighing up the answers to all of the above, should I let the play continue or step in to stop or change what she is doing?

And yes, I do realise that it's a lot to think about in a very short space of time – it's not called *speed-of-light risk assessment* for nothing, you know!

Of course there will be some situations where you know straight away that a large amount of harm is going to happen very soon if you don't step in right now – sometimes we don't have time to get to the third bullet point before stepping in to put a stop to something, let alone the last one!

However, there will also be situations where you decide not to get involved because you can see that to do so would be to put a stop to the benefits of the play for very little reason. A child tying up another child with a skipping rope might not be in danger of causing a significant amount of harm if both children look happy with it, the rope is round a part of the body that isn't going to put a stop to breathing and, from their point of view, having reins on your horse is essential for going on an adventure!

There might be other situations where you can help children to continue playing but introduce a couple of modifications to lessen the likelihood of harm occurring. In the case of children who are playing rough and tumble, for example, you might be able to get them to play on a softer surface so that they're minimising the risk of landing hard. Sure, they still might get a couple of bruises, but you might decide that the harm that this could do to them is fairly minimal given the benefits of rough-and-tumble play.

And of course there will always be situations when adults intervening could potentially increase the risk of children getting hurt. Shouting at the child who is standing on the swinging gate to get off, for example, may not be the best thing to do when he may be using all his powers of concentration to stay balanced! Sometimes one of the ways that you can ensure that risk in play stays within acceptable limits is just by watching how something is developing – and doing *speed-of-light risk assessments* whilst you're observing!

Remember that risk is relative – we all have our own comfort zones – and children are no different. Risk is not only relative to who the child is, but also to the circumstances, so the level of risk needs to be assessed in those specific circumstances. So you will need to go through the same *speed-of-light risk assessment* process each time that same situation occurs but the circumstances are different – for example:

- different children – children have different levels of confidence and ability when it comes to risk

- different weather conditions – the level of risk will be different for some types of play in dry or wet conditions, for example

- different moods of the children – children who come to your setting hyped up after a bad day at school are possibly not going to be as receptive to safety instructions as when they are in a calm frame of mind.

In other words, just because you judge it's safe enough for Fred to swing on that particular gate today, doesn't automatically mean that Johnny will be allowed to do the same thing tomorrow. Risk assessment when it comes to children's play is not a scientific process – it really does all depend.

So I hope by now that you will see why those 110 commandments (that number isn't a typo by the way – there do seem to be an awful lot of them!) when it comes to risk in play just don't work. You know the ones – no running, no waving sticks, no getting out of sight of adults, no throwing things… There may be times when all of these things could indeed prove an unacceptable level of risk to the children in your setting, but there will also be times when all of those things are not only vitally important to children's play, but also present a low level of risk. Risk assessments (and remembering to put the benefits in there when appropriate) help us to decide where we should – and should not – draw that line.

Minimising risk

When you do decide that you need to minimise the risk of harm taking place, there are several things that you can do (and probably do already), but you may not think of these things as part of a risk assessment. These might include:

- talking to children

- site checks

- providing extra equipment (like crashmats or protective clothing)

- mending/cleaning/throwing out equipment

- checking for quality standards on equipment

- site visits.

These things all form part of your risk assessment – some of it may seem like that mythical *common sense*, but they all count as things you might do to help keep children safe enough in your setting.

Just a small word of caution on talking to children before we move on – let's remember that the whole point of talking to children about hazards is to make them aware of things they might not have been aware of, and/or to help them to weigh up risks for themselves, and/or to give them clear and age-appropriate information as to why you have decided the risk is too high for them to take part in certain forms of play. The point of talking to children is *not* to scare them witless about just how much harm they might come to so that they never go anywhere near that particular thing again! It's all very well subjecting three-year-olds to a 15-minute lecture on the dangers of brambles, thistles, nettles, holes, wasps, bees, bumping into each other, tripping over low branches and getting splinters – but if that means that they are too frightened to go anywhere near the great outdoors ever again, then it sort of defeats the object, doesn't it!? (Believe me, it happens – we're currently developing a weird breed of pre-schoolers who will on no account go near anything that's vaguely green – all in the name of *health and safety*…)

Recording risk assessments

And yes, of course – I've saved the best until last – but it might not be as bad as you think, honest! The HSE reminds us that 'A risk assessment is not about creating huge amounts of paperwork, but rather about identifying sensible measures to control the risks in your workplace', and that we should record 'significant findings'. Please note that it does not tell us to fill out a 64-page manual each time a child sets one foot outdoors or on a chair. Once again, it's up to you to decide what's 'suitable and sufficient' when it comes to recording your risk assessments and your risk–benefit decisions.

Of course some settings will work in the context of larger organisations – for example, settings linked to the local authority, nursery chains, etc. These umbrella organisations may publish their own procedures and documents for recording risk assessments, in which case it's important to be aware of what your employer requires you to do. However, it's also important to remember that these procedures will not be the only (or even *right*) way to do risk assessments, which may be done or recorded differently in other settings. There are risk assessment templates on the HSE website which may be helpful in recording your risk assessments, but it's also important to remember that, because the law leaves it to us to decide what is 'suitable and sufficient', any templates or models must be 'suitable and sufficient' for your setting.

However you decide to record your risk assessments, find a way which can be used by the whole team as part of your regular routines in your setting. And don't forget to record some of those *speed-of-light risk–benefit assessments* too. There's no need to go mad and write down every single risk–benefit assessment that goes through your head (that really would drive you mad!). However, making a few notes at the end of each session could be helpful when it comes to those team discussions about risk, and could also demonstrate that you are making informed decisions about risk in play, rather than just making it up as you go along!

The benefits of risk assessment

So, there you have it – risk assessment can actually be a tool to help us to facilitate (rather than just automatically ban different types of) play. Hoorah for risk assessment, I say!

As we come to the end of *The Busker's Guide to Risk*, risk should no longer be a four-letter word when it comes to children's play. Armed with some careful thinking about the benefits of play to children, a clear understanding of what the law requires (rather than what *they* do or tell you to do), and a risk assessment process which is 'suitable and sufficient' for your setting, I hope we can now put our fear of risk in play in perspective. Have fun, folks – and I really do mean that!

And Finally...

There are always a couple of things that come up in training courses about risk and play...so I've included them here in the hope that they answer some questions for you too!

> *Our mission statement says that our setting is safe, happy and friendly... – can we not say that any more then?*

Well...I wouldn't say you can't...it's just that I wouldn't. For a start, the concept of *safety* (absence of danger) is difficult in children's play. Children have a great knack of tripping over fresh air when they are hardly moving, so promising parents that no harm will come to their little darlings when they are doing what comes naturally to them in your settings (i.e. playing) is only going to encourage parents to expect what cannot be true – and this could mean that they'll give you more flak when they find out you've been fibbing... Second, this is a great opportunity we're missing out on here to let parents know about the importance of play in helping children to learn how to make risk assessments for themselves. So I'd say something like *safe enough*, or *appropriately safe* instead – and then be prepared to explain what this means. You could do this in a play policy which gives details of the sorts of play that your setting supports, and why (yes, I know, more paperwork – but it might save you from some of that flak in the long run…!).

So that's great – we'll do pages and pages of risk assessments and then we won't get sued?

Ah – no, sorry! Whilst we can probably go as far as saying that people don't get found guilty in a court of law for children having accidents, they do get into trouble for being negligent. Risk assessments can certainly help you to demonstrate that you've thought about the potential hazards in any situation, and that you've done what you felt was 'reasonably practicable' to minimise the risks. But just because you do a risk assessment doesn't mean you won't get sued – because if decisions were not very well thought out or not 'suitable and sufficient' then you could be found negligent. Remember that when it comes to making risk assessments, quantity is not necessarily the same as quality – it's more important to be able to clearly explain the decisions you made and why you made them, than how many pages of pretty bar charts you produce. As the HSE says, 'keep it simple'.

Further Reading

These resources can all be downloaded for free from the internet. Simply put the details below into your favourite search engine, or find the links at: www.jkp.com/catalogue/book/9781849056823/resources.

Ball, D., Gill, T. and Spiegal, B. (2012) *Managing Risk in Play Provision: Implementation Guide*. London: National Children's Bureau.

Barnardos (2011) *Children's Risky Play*. ChildLinks, Issue 3.

Gleave, J. (2008) *Risk and Play: A Literature Review*. Published for Play England by the National Children's Bureau.

Health and Safety Executive (2014) *Risk Assessment: A Brief Guide to Controlling Risks in the Workplace*.

Health and Safety Executive (2012) *Children's Play and Leisure – Promoting a Balanced Approach*.

Play Wales (2008) *A Playworker's Guide to Risk*.